growing light

alaska gold

Copyright © 2015 by Alaska Gold

All rights reserved. This book or any portion thereof may not be reproduced or used in any manner whatsoever without the express written permission of the publisher except for the use of brief quotations in a book review or scholarly journal.

ISBN: 1495322009

ISBN-13: 978-1495322006

Cover Design by Alaska Gold © 2015

For us

*If the boy who draws
lets you look over his shoulder.
If the poet
smiles
and shows you her words.
If the girl who sings for the shower only,
hums a song
in front of you.
Know that you're no longer a person
but the air
and dust
that fills their lungs.
When the world perishes,
and all things cease to exist,
you'll remain inside an ink stain,
a paint brush,
a song.*

Poem N. 8

PART ONE

There was only darkness at first. We drifted, waited. Two bodies. Eyes closed. This is how language found us, how it taught us new ways to pronounce home. Some wars are fought in houses too. This is how they took our light away. How we learned to grow without it. These are our lips moving. That noise——our stories breathing for the first time.

Come closer, let us tell you face to face.
Let us tell you poem to poem.

We write
to become children again.

The doctors flinched
when they pulled us from the womb.
We were children bred from fire,
conceived by adventures and born
with a growing need to be everywhere.

They described us as bad habits with good intentions
because we kissed until our bones would break
and weren't scared of being born again.

We weren't people.
We were wildfire with flesh
learning how to burn.

When they came knocking on our door
we set the house on fire.
What they found is all we left behind.

Birthing flames

There are houses that never stop shouting,
rooms that don't know how to calm down.
So you grew up carrying your smile
on a string around your neck,
where they wouldn't see
and never take it.

I touch you
and stain my hands with light,
and that's how I know
the sun sleeps somewhere inside you.

When the stars look at you with dread
and our mother breathes with the intent
to blow out your fire,
I will take the earth of your hands into my own
and teach you to grow with your eyes closed.

I will never give you the things
our parents
gave to me.

Promises

The first time I licked a man's chapped lips,
he fisted his hands between my bones
to keep me from running.

So many thought
they could eat up the darkness
tucked away behind my teeth.

You wouldn't think so,
but my body is a disaster zone,
an 8.1 on the Richter scale.

Honey, there's no hope for survival.

This is not the place for you

You grew so used to destruction,
even *I love you*
feels like violence
to your heart.

Brittle truths

The day I slept with the boy
who majored in mathematics
I didn't leave right away.

Before we kissed,
he paused to calculate the coordinates
of where our lips would meet.

He explained why x tends to infinity
in the same way I tend to break hearts.
And concluded I had an asymptotic behaviour;
try as they might, I never let men touch me.

He worked out the function for how to hold me,
close enough so there'd be no open space
and the exact number of laughs
that would fill in my empty cracks.

I pulled him close one night to say,
not even boys like you
can work out how to solve me.

Function for a tender heart

It's a lonely thing
keeping your heart from breaking.

Remaining whole

She met a boy
and called him Stargazer
because instead of poems
he recited the names of constellations.

He said the freckles on his arms
were roadmaps to the sky,
and the bruises that he carried
were supernovas in disguise.

Stargazer

When I first met Finn he brought his index finger to his lips
and let it slide, forming two circles over his mouth.

This meant lonely in sign language.

In middle school he wrote Canberra on his hands
because no one seemed to remember Australia's capital city.
He confessed to have measured his sorrow
into a coffee mug, only to realize fifty sugar cubes later
he still tasted bittersweet.

Fin never said *I love you*, instead he said *I need you*.
Especially at night, when his arms held on to me
for dear life.

>He inhaled.

>I exhaled.

And saved him
from holding his breath.

Early-onset loneliness

I was told a story of a boy and a girl
who carried silver strings inside of them,
to hold their life together.

Some nights the boy would fall into bed
and drown himself
in tears.

He grew the habit of cutting
the ends of his life string,
as an attempt to wipe away his sadness.

What he never knew
was the girl did the same.
Every morning she cut from her string
a thread the size of her finger
and sowed it back to his.

I asked people if the boy was mad.
They said he was.
I asked about the girl,
they said
        she was in love.

Breaking myself
so we're broken together

The storm keeps knocking on our door
and I'm awake to keep you from opening it.
This is the price of growing with outstretched arms;
of giving until you can't tell who last borrowed your heart.

You have been wrecked by all who love you
and taught to love them still.

So many have welcomed you with open arms
and open scars, expecting you to beat their hearts.
And you,
have returned home with holes
in every place they touched you.

Loving hurts you in all the ways it shouldn't.

So here I am
trying to take you back from giving.
Collecting all the pieces you gave away
and feeding them back to you in the right order.

Let me hold you in my palm
and breathe into your soul.
Let me warm you from the inside and
write you a new word for love.

The road back from giving

He carries stars in his pockets
because he knows
she fears the dark.
Whenever sadness pays her a visit
he paints galaxies
on the back of her hands.

N. 16

The neighbours won't meet our eyes anymore.
They look away, scared the youth in our hearts
will be contagious.

It's dark when we arrive, it's 2am
and we haven't paid the light bill.
So we make our way through the house
using our mouths.

My hands forget what they are when they touch you,
my fingers ache
for a place they're not meant to reach.
And the truth is that you are so much
I find it hard to breathe sometimes.

I left the window open somewhere
in the second story of my heart
and you dragged along the sinew,
passed the dark and bone
certain you'd find a place of your own.

You burn so bright I've begun to call you morning.
So if you leave
       please,
              don't take the sunlight with you.

House of the sun

Things get to you so easily these days.
There was a time when you could speak
without anger in your mouth,
breathe without soot marrying your hands.

This was a poem about forgiveness
but you lost your way.
Forgot how to turn yourself
back into a child again.

When mothers leave, the secret
is learning how to let them.
Sometimes they don't know where they hurt
and so they make you pain—
make you something ugly.

There are mothers who spend
their whole life howling
but even they
give birth to children too.

What it took to understand

You were awake when war slipped under your door
and took the shape of bank bills and heart failures.
These are the stories you hid beneath your tongue,
and how you learned to smile
without anyone finding them.

How often was it night time with you
barring all the windows of your home
so they wouldn't smell the burning inside?

You slipped the child out of your soul and put it to rest.
You promised to return one day
but you had bones to break and lessons to learn,
and you couldn't let it be ruined.

This is how you pushed everyone out. This is
how you kept alive.
You let go of all the people you loved
and some did not forgive you.

But when the storm finally walks home
and the sun dries the water in your lungs,
you'll return to where you left your soul.

Soft and warm, it won't fit your chest anymore.

You will leave it behind,
and this is how you'll save it.

Sound of survival

It took fifty seven days to find your smile
after the waves washed it away.
This is what we call misplacement;
how we leave our hearts by the door
so they remain tender.

Things have been wrong for so long
you think it somehow makes them right.
So you keep trading your bones
for broken glass,
keep taking too much of the world
into your hands.

You shouldn't have grown this old so young.

Listen.
I will lose myself
if it means I can find you.

All this time I've been trying to build
something bright enough
to save us both.

Just wait.
That place will be wonderful.
Someday, for sure.

A poem to call home

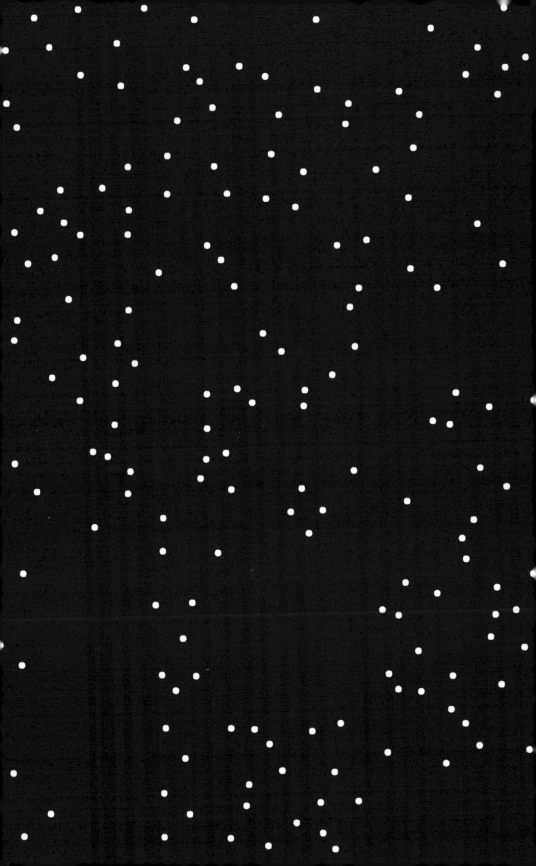

PART TWO

That's when my heart heard yours, and went:
  "*I've been waiting for you.*
      Please, stay a while."

Exist with me, we'd do so beautifully.

During the time it takes for you to reach your napkin,
I've memorized the contour of your hand
and you think I'm trembling because I'm cold
but I'm just keeping myself from touching you.

I must've swallowed truth for breakfast,
because nothing else explains
why I called you a gasoline spill on the pavement
or mentioned your pomegranate heart.

You sound a whole lot like early mornings
and sunshine filtering through curtains,
and all I can think of
is how much I need to hold your hair
between my stiff fingers,
because your body is a safety line
and I've been adrift for too long.

You smile in time with my rambling, your eyes
creasing a little at the sides.
And before I can think twice about it, I confess
I'm jealous of the mark you left on the wine glass
because I want that imprint on my neck.

I'm running out of things to say already
and they haven't brought the main course yet.
So when you take it upon yourself to speak instead
I'm surprised of the way you use your lips,
because unlike me, you don't make a sound.

Example of a better way to speak

I need you to love me the same way
the moon orbits around the earth,
without intention to stop.

Confessing the heart

My father cares for a woman that isn't my mother
because what comes first isn't always best.
He loves a woman he cannot touch,
he cannot smell and cannot taste.
Like the moon and sun, they're not meant
to be in the same place at once.

Their love is a long distance runner;
an inexperienced traveller
that forgets his passport home.

They measure miles in heartbeats
because what they hold is so big
it cannot fit in this house,
nor in this street,
not even in this country.

Perhaps something this tender needs oceans to bloom
and countries to grow, and distance
is just an excuse to love harder.

Long distance runners

It's 5 am and I heard summer slip under the door. I'm going to wake up soon because I feel your breath on my arm and I want to check if your hair is still soft. You look so pretty right now I want to drink tea, and the truth is I really want to kiss you to make sure I do it right. Somewhere here I'll write something that makes sense. Don't wake up yet, let me practice one more time.

Some nights I stay awake to help you dream

It's spring and you don't feel lovable anymore,
you haven't felt so in a long time.
Your name leaves a bad taste in your mouth
and though I'm trying to kiss you better,
it's time you stop throwing your body
out the window
and teach it how to use the stairs.

I don't want to save you.

I want to hold your hand
and watch you do the saving.

But maybe you're right and the stars
are a little too high to reach for tonight.
All I know is tomorrow we'll keep trying.

I'm starting to think this was never a poem
but a promise.

Late blooming

You speak in flowers
and sometimes I don't reply
because I can't bring myself to ruin
something so beautiful.

The secrets we keep

You are playing with your hands and I'm fighting the urge to cross the room and ask you the time, because my watch stopped working the moment I saw you. My knees are shaking in beat with your heart, and if you were to look at me you'd hear all the questions I'm piling under my tongue; *Where is your home? Are you waiting for someone? Would you like to fall in love?*

You are sitting now, with your elbows apart and smiling to yourself. I should tell you I am writing this about you. But you are looking so real that I don't want to disrupt everything you are. All I hope is you feel these words running like fingers through your hair, and if ever your heart sinks into your stomach trust these lines to put it back in place.

You order your bill and shift to the side. This is the first and last time I will see you. So excuse me for being so emotionally blunt, but there's a part of me that already loves you.

Here's where it happened

We are not in love.
But if we were,
oh, we'd make it beautiful.

Allow me this

Lately you've been coughing up empty poems
without showing signs of stopping.
You've been sleeping with letters
and running away in the mornings,
too scared after not loving them properly.

You're trying to pack your heart into words again
but your hands tremble every time you hold a pen.
You either write in even breaths
or to the point of suffocation.
There's nothing in between.

You're a world trapped under skin and bone.
You are words; red and pulsing
asking for a home.

But when the poems decide to leave—let them.
They will run and go places.
They will write worlds without you.

Ignore the burning in your hands.
Say you'll miss them, say
love is not measured by the willingness to stay
but the decision to come back.

It wasn't the writing, it was me

Two months after our break up
I was still searching for you in the mouths of other men.
The same who gave away kisses like spare change,
and sleep walked out of buildings with their zippers undone.

You had wanted to carve my love bites onto your skin
to decipher my body's words. All because you thought
it took skill to become fluent in someone,
and you wished for me to be your mother tongue.

I guess it's true what the moon told me;
once you learn to speak a language
there are words you can't forget.
It must explain why even two months later
whenever I try to say *I love you,*
all I manage is your name.

Love and other foreign languages

The moon feared the dark,
so the sun
set himself on fire.

How day came to be

On our first night together
we set the garden ablaze
and scorched the walls of the bedroom.

I remember you fit your hands
inside my bones
as we rose higher and higher.

You confessed to being scared of the fall,
so I kissed you, filling myself with all of you
to burn away your doubts and fears.

When the police stormed the apartment,
I asked them what the crime was
in loving someone so much
even the earth rose up in flames.

La petite mort

When I'm mad at you I won't talk to you. I'll huddle on my side of the bed, wait until you're out of the kitchen, avoid your name if I can. I'll be mad, but I'll make sure there's enough milk for you in the mornings. I'll be mad, and so I'll love you quietly.

*I love you,
but leave me alone*

You cradle my face when we kiss
because we make it rough and dangerous;
we kiss like a damn breaking
and we're not scared of running out of breath.

We sound a lot like thunderstorms,
like shattered glass and desperation.

We're so close you may as well be holding
my skin together, but no matter how deep
you sink your hands, no matter
how hard our teeth may clash,
your hands on my face remind me
you're nothing but gentle with my love.

*Our breathing
fogged the sky for days*

I must've lost my underwear in your bed
or misplaced it on the counter. But either way
all I kept thinking was I should've kissed you longer.

I kept from looking at you the next day
because the only way I want to see your eyes
is with the lights off.

You never knew, but I was so full of love
I spilled on the sheets, and I couldn't help
to love you desperately
because that's the only way I knew.

I was never good at math but somewhere I've read
two negatives make a positive.
I may be mistaken, but if so
I'd like to be a mistake with you.

Come over,
I want to fall in love

I think the stars are smart
for being far away.
We can't ruin them that way.

This could be about us

I'm calling to say I haven't slept on my bed tonight
because the sheets still show the skin maps of your body,
and I'm trying very hard not to breathe because
I don't want to wake them up.

If your body were a question mark
I wouldn't be the right answer.

I'm only good at loving carelessly, but I called
because I want to change my ways.
I want to love you capital letters, love you bridges,
love you rainy pavements and flushed skin.

This city isn't our own.
This bed, this room, isn't our own
but I want you to be.
Because I've heard them say home is where you're wanted.

I'm one sentence away from falling asleep
and all I can think of is how much I want to taste
last night on your tongue again. And although
I tried my best not to fall in love with you,
you made it really hard.

While our story would be one of destruction,
it'd be the prettiest ever told.

Hi, it's me

PART THREE

One time we packed our bodies into a suitcase and returned for a day. Every breath reminded us of all the hurt we'd buried here. Except there was nothing waiting for us anymore. We realized then, everything had vanished after we left. We had saved ourselves but hadn't saved this place.

Only this time it found us. Small and pulsing—it had worn out with time, but felt strangely familiar. We held it to our chest, felt it smile against our flesh.

We called it *forgiveness*.

Don't wait for spring to come.
Become.

My father takes my hands and traces
the lines on my palms with his fingers.
He says, we are mistakes
trying to be wonderful.

We grow up, and ashamed of things that break—
shattered plates, snapped pencils, even
ourselves. We're afraid to learn
how to piece our bodies back together.
So we hide under sheets, flush mistakes
down the toilet, pretend
we don't bleed.

But in Japan they know different; there
they join your broken bones
with powdered gold and lacquer.
Call it kintsugi, call it I broke down
and forgave myself. These scars say
I can breathe despite the damage.

So take your own hand,
you are fragile but filled with hope.
These cracks are your story
and you tell it so well.

Golden joinery

Look at you, so full of light.
Not afraid to get burned,
not afraid to burn out.

You live and do it so well

Some days you're nineteen and forget who you are. You remember to pick up the dry cleaning, yet you've forgotten where your eyes are on your face. You're worried you don't have thoughts on God or politics and don't make for an interesting person. All you've got is a talent you try too hard to tame.

Some days you're nineteen and forget what you lived for. You knew life was too short to pause halfway to sit and breathe. So you woke up wanting to become someone else, and be somewhere else. You wanted to be called an adventure. But nowadays, you kiss with your mouth closed and don't wear your heart anymore.

Some days you're nineteen and forget how young that is. You forget you're still growing. That you can smile with your teeth, be dark and lazy and get drunk after no more than two sips of gin. You're uncertain, untouched and unprepared and you are yours before ever anyone else's. So it's alright if some days you're not ready. It's alright that you're still learning. You're alright.

*This is for you
more than anyone else*

When I caught the taste of sunshine between your teeth
you warned me that we wouldn't last much longer
because you couldn't help but fall in love with many things.

You were taught to live desperately,
to think recklessly,
to speak with an accent full of love and carry
your heart in your hands.

When the doctors pulled you from the womb
they searched your mother's legs for ashes
because you burned with the heat of a thousand suns.

You grew up hanging lanterns on hilltops to make sure
the moon could see at night, and practiced
catching droplets of rain with your lips,
because even clouds deserved a little romance.

They'll throw faulty smiles and promises without refunds
at your feet, and expect you to carry yourself like an apology.
Just remember that no matter how soft they make you speak
your eyes will never grow quiet.

Like a true child of nature,
you were born to be wild.

*I wrote her a poem
but I'm not Mars Bonfire*

You made me write down the instructions
on how to braid strands of confidence into your hair
before you left to college.

I promised to email you at 6:20 every afternoon,
as a reminder that you're 620 miles away from home.

You will have days when you'll want
to build a storm shelter in bed,
when people kiss your cheeks
and wonder at the saltiness.
They'll ask how you lost your voice
and you'll reply it's nothing but a sad throat.

You will call home, needing someone to hear you cry,
honey, that's alright.
Remember clouds don't have anyone
who wipes away their tears,
and even the moon hides her face once a month.

Understand that cracking your bones
doesn't mean you're close to breaking.

I'll say it once more,
darling, it's okay to grow up.

For when her bones stop growing

She is going to walk through that door;
a mess of smiles and rain-kissed hair,
and you're going to want her.
Want her name in your mouth, her hands on your heart.
But you will have to wait. She's not the person
you are meant to love yet.

She's got to fumble on her own first,
show others the pink in her mouth and spring
in her heart. She's going to take sadness to bed
and call it intimate. Call it loving.

She's going to hurt.

And yet
she's going to make herself smile
so you can smile together.

No matter how angry the storm, the waves always
hug the shore. Eventually people return home.
Scraped knees and purple under her eyes;
she's going to come back.
She'll smile something like heartbreak,
say, *look at you, look at you,*
I've been growing my heart for yours.

Saving us for when we're better

When my friends asked why I was called Andromeda,
I told them my father was an astronaut.

I came from school one day,
and found him painting my bedroom wall
in black. That night
we used white chalk
to draw the stars outside my window.

He carried two things in his pockets:
a ripped paper with my name,
and a tiny bottle of cough pills.

I went off to college,
but didn't study astronomy.
By then I understood
the scratches on my father's wrists
weren't tallies of all the times he'd danced
with the moon.

However, if you ask me
what my father's dream was,
I'd say it was to be an astronaut
and in my eyes,
he was.

The astronaut's daughter

You spend your savings on paperclip bones
and trade your smiles for others that wont falter in the dark.
Every breath you take is self-destructive, and you still
bite the skin off your fingers and set yourself on fire,
because you haven't learned to love yourself correctly.

It may be difficult to love everything you are
but when your mind feeds you poison as milk,
remember that your body
is the one to hold you in its arms.

You are naked skin and colours without a name.
Take up space at the dinner table,
sit with open eyes and your elbows apart
because your existence isn't an apology letter.

Love yourself harder than you've ever loved anyone else
and stop wishing for negative space between your bones.

This body was made to carry a heart the size of yours.

You haven't realized yet
but inside you
is everything you need to be happy.

Learning to love by example

For longer than I would like to admit
I thought I could exist somewhere inside you.
I hid my heart in your heart
and mixed them up
until there was only one beating.

This is how I lied to myself;
how I drowned with your mouth on my mouth,
thinking we were making something beautiful.

We could be happy again
but not together.

I heard spring could make things wonderful again.
But the truth is I was already wondrous
before I met you.

The truth is
so were you.

All along I've been trying to forgive you
and forgive myself,
for loving at a time
when there was too much growing left to do.

I'm sorry,
I couldn't save you for later.

Thank you for loving me

He loved her
but he was like the sun.
He couldn't shine for her alone.

Lessons in heartbreak

He needed some space, time to remember how to hold her again. You will fall in love with people, and sometimes they will fall in love with you. Do not settle here. They must love you all at once; think of losing your breath, think of dawn breaking. When the stars fall from your eyes and the ones you trusted pull their hands away, remember you're a light learning to burn and those hands aren't set to hold you. Do not let your fire dwindle for those too scared to touch you.

You will be the light

At my worst,
I burned the brightest.

Icarus

Stop checking your pockets whenever you feel heavy hearted,
it's not the receipts and spare change weighing you down.
Sometimes you've carried feelings for so long,
they ink onto your skin.

I heard you're an expert at peeling away emotions
and leaving them on a pile beside stranger's beds.

You shouldn't have to do this.

They should've taught you how to breathe properly;
how to exhale sadness using your lungs.

Remember why solar eclipses occur;
the moon hides the sun from sight
so we do not see it shed tears.

I'm sure even autumn leaves wish
they wouldn't grow back in spring.

Start viewing the ocean as half-full
and washing your hands to get rid of your sorrow.

It's time you learn to treat
the scars on your body like an anagram.
If you arrange the markings on your skin
you will hear your body whisper,
     I survived.

Becoming true again

I love you.
I'm not so good at it, but I do.
I do.

Words to myself

Today, peal the sleep away from your eyes and tuck it under your pillow. When you get out of bed, stand on your toes and kiss the sun good morning, hard enough to shock the clouds nearby. Remember to hug your mother today. Lay a hand on her stomach because that was the first place you ever called home. Before you leave the house, uncover one of your mirrors. People say you have your father's teeth, so wear that knowledge like a medallion and smile at yourself today. Don't try to brush out the tangles in your hair. You are the child of two dreamers; carry yourself a little taller today and flirt with the stars just to see if they blush easily.

Walk on light feet and speak using a needle and thread so your words are better remembered. Go out on your best dress and sing to yourself out of tune. People will stare at you, some will try to bleed you dry but don't let their darkness reach you. Today you're a sky lantern. When they throw heartbreak and disappointment at your feet, and the world ties your shoelaces together, remember that fireflies are the size of paperclips and yet they are confused with stars, which tells you it doesn't take a big heart to light up the earth.

Today, tell yourself it'll be a good day

EPILOGUE

Eventually we ran out of words to write.
So we swallowed the stars,
and there was nothing but light
        when they found us.

THE BLAME FOR THIS BOOK GOES TO:

The *boy who draws*, with whom all of this started.

To all my readers from Tumblr— for reading these poems long before they existed on paper. Thank you for your messages, your art, and endless encouragement. I'm honored to have you with me.

To Charlie Howard, for her unending faith, and everyone who has a handmade collection of their own. Thank you.

To Claudia, who probably won't know about this book until she finds her phone again. But who's championed my writing long before I did.

To my sister, Ale. Thank you for growing up with me. I'm sorry I bribed you to read each piece in this book over and over. I promise the next one will be about crickets.

Finally, thank you to all of you who inspired this, but will never know it exists.